THE SANDS OF TIME

Stoney-Baynard Ruins

A HISTORY OF
HILTON HEAD ISLAND

BY MARGARET GREER

ACKNOWLEDGEMENTS

A recorder of history has generations of acknowledgements to express. My appreciation goes to those who have previously kept the record of historic events in this intriguing area. In particular I would like to thank Mr. and Mrs. Charles E. Fraser for allowing their extensive collection of maps and photographs to be used; Mrs. Fred C. Hack and Orion Hack for their recollections; Mike Taylor, director of the Hilton Head Island Environmental and Historical Museum; the staff of The South Carolina Historical Society in Charleston; and my husband, Walter Greer, for suggestions and encouragement, and for the reproduction rights to his painting.

CREDITS FOR ILLUSTRATIONS

South Carolina Historical Society, *Pages 30, 37*

Charles E. Fraser, *Pages 4, 11, 16, 19, 28, 39, 40, 41, 45, 46, 47, 49, 53, 59*

Hilton Head Island Environmental and Historical Museum, *Pages 57, 58*

Mrs. Frederick C. Hack, *Page 23*

United States Marine Corps, Parris Island Museum, *Page 7*, Painting by Scott B. Krouse and map, *Page 14*

Walter Greer, *Page 15*

William Cornelia, *Color photographs*

Prologue

Hilton Head is more than just another resort or burgeoning town by the sea. She is a lady with a past, a lady who is beautiful, sometimes sinful, always controversial, and who continues to keep a few secrets. This makes her all the more intriguing and causes people to return again and again if they cannot linger for a lifetime.

The ruins of old plantations, Indian shell rings, the mystery of a mausoleum, the tales of ghosts and the lyrics of the Gullah language all beg for more exploration and information. The quest goes on. Archaeologists and historians are finding answers.

Although three books on Island history have been published, one dealing exclusively with the Civil War on Hilton Head, new information requires that another book be written and, as secrets held for hundreds of years yield to the scholar, more books will be forthcoming.

The Island has been a frontier of Spain, a colony of France, a pivotal and strategic base of operations early in the Civil War, and a strong force in the economic resurgence of the South.

Over four hundred years ago, Spaniards from the West Indies brought living cargo that became Hilton Head's heritage: Negro slaves, the first of many whose descendants became landowners; Dominican monks who blazed tree trunks with the Cross of Christ; and almost one hundred Spanish horses whose sturdy traits are still visible in the tethered Marsh Tackies prized by Gullah natives.

Until the English established permanency, the Island was used then as it is today — a happy hunting ground. Indians, Spanish, French, and English all agreed on two things: the land was fertile, and the water was fresh. Fresh water is as precious as gold to the sailor. Old maps mark two sites with the words "aqua dulce" or "eau douce" at Spanish Wells and also near Skull Creek Village.

The estuaries and creeks not only hid pirates long ago, but also harbored bootleggers during prohibition and, more recently, drug smugglers. The famous High Sheriff of the Low Country, Ed McTeer, suggested that his department needed fast boats instead of fast cars. "Careening Point" is another designation on old charts. Did pirates careen their boats for a cleaning here? Is this why a nearby place on Skull Creek is labeled Golgotha? Skull and crossbones. Golgotha — place of the skulls. Is this why the creek on the northwest side of Hilton Head is called Skull, or is it called by that name because Indians used to "skulk" along the shore and prey upon settlers? History can be as vibrant as your imagination.

Hilton Head Island can claim many "firsts," most of them occurring during or because of the Civil War, or, as the Negroes called it, "When Gun Shoot." Certainly there has been more written history about this period of Island life than any other. Port Royal was the site of the largest naval operation to that date mounted by the United States government. And it was the site of the first American amphibious landing. The first Negro troops were mustered here, and although it was retracted, the first proclamation freeing the slaves was issued on Hilton Head long before President Lincoln was ready to do so. Over a hundred years later the first ecological battle, in which a small group of citizens defeated a large polluting industry, took place on this Island.

Whatever else may be said of history, one thing remains. History is hope. If we do not know yesterday and remember it, how can we imagine tomorrow? Hilton Head Island has much history. Eras are interwoven and dependent upon each other. Through the centuries those who have come here seeking sustenance or wealth or restoration, all know that they have found a truly beautiful and remarkable part of the earth.

Charles Nordhoff's description for *Harper's New Monthly Magazine*, written in 1863, applies equally well for today. "I thought, Hither one might come, weary of the busy world, and live contented forever — nor ever long for a New York Paper..."

Margaret Greer
Hilton Head Island, S.C.
September 5, 1988

Table of Contents

"If you could have asked a local resident (in whatever form) to direct you to the ocean, he would have pointed to the rising sun and told you to prepare for a journey of a little over three hundred miles."

CHAPTER I

The Land Made Ready

*T*en thousand years ago Hilton Head was not an island. The entire area was a river valley, good hunting for the nomadic Paleo-Indians.

If you could have visited Hilton Head 25,000 years ago, the foliage and trees would have resembled those of today's state of Maine. The temperature of the ocean only reached 53 degrees Fahrenheit in the summer. If you could have asked a local resident (in whatever form) to direct you to the ocean, he would have pointed to the rising sun and told you to prepare for a journey of over three hundred miles.

So it was 25,000 years ago, but a warming trend melted glaciers and the sea level rose westward toward the present coastline. Faced with mounting pressures of the Beaufort and Broad rivers which feed Port Royal Sound to the north, the May and Cooper rivers creating Calibogue Sound, Hilton Head at last became an island.

Before our Epoch there was the Pleistocene Epoch which was marked by four major Ice Ages. As each glacier formed, our hemisphere was scraped, gouged, and re-shaped as ice advanced and retreated over land and ocean basin alike. Hilton Head Island has a Pleistocene core with a Holocene beach ridge fringe although high sea level stands constructed dune ridges which are evident over most of the Island.

The present period is warm and northern glaciers continue to melt. All along the coasts of the United States, gauges of the Coast and Geodetic Survey have recorded a rise in Sea Level since 1930.

Repeated coastal inundations and ups and down of tidal fluctuations during the Holocene Epoch have sculptured the Island as it is today — with the exceptions of many developers and a few golf course architects. Low sea levels are recorded at 1860 B.C. at *minus* 10.6 feet. By A.D. 1650, about the time the English were getting interested in Carolina, the sea level of Hilton Head Island was only about 2.6 feet lower than it is today. The land was ready for history.

CHAPTER II
The Indians

Ten to fourteen thousand years ago, in what was then a fertile river valley, the Paleo-Indians roamed the area that incorporates Hilton Head Island. Years ago this relatively small group had already attained what so many people strive for today: a short work week, uncrowded conditions, a ready food source, a boat, abundant hunting and fishing, moderate climate, travel, and no mortgage.

". . .they found about 2,000 Indians known as Escamacu, ruled by chiefs, who used all the islands as hunting grounds. . ."

Artifacts found here and along major river drainages in the Low Country indicate these Indians hunted the "now extinct mega-fauna."

During the Archaic period, 8,000 to 2,000 B.C., the Indians continued their high mobility, but it is the succeeding Woodland period that is documented along the South Carolina coast. The period begins with fired clay pottery about 2,000 B.C. Subsistence living, imitated in part by the abandoned Negroes after the Civil War, was based on hunting, fishing and harvesting shellfish. Various shell ring sites near waterways tell us that Woodland Indians had settled down.

Shell rings were formed by accumulation of shellfish in a circular pattern measuring several hundred feet in diameter and up to ten feet in height. The mystery of why these rings were built still remains although theorizing continues. One belief is that Indians lived within these rings, keeping the interiors clear for communal activities. Others contend the rings were for ceremonial purposes only. One such example of a shell ring may be seen on Squire Pope Road on private property across from the tabby remains of an ante-bellum plantation "business" building which is believed to have been partially built with shells from the nearby ring. The other Island shell ring, as full of mystery as Stonehenge, is in the Sea Pines Forest Preserve.

The Middle and Late Woodland period lasted until 1000 A.D. and indicates seasonal occupancy of Hilton Head Island, most probably in fall and winter. Not too different from fortunate modern residents who have summer places elsewhere. In a 1986 archaeological "dig" sponsored by the Museum of Hilton Head small campsite remains were discovered. The pattern of an Indian house, probably dating about 1300 B.C. was found intact in the soil on the north end of the Island at the Fish Haul site.

The Mississippian period follows and brings the Indian in this area to the beginning of written history and to his nemesis — the advent of the European. When Spaniards sailing from Santo Domingo in 1526 came upon the islands of Port Royal, they found about 2,000 Indians known as the Escamacu, ruled by chiefs, who used all the islands as hunting grounds seasonally. They had built settlements of round thatched houses and apparently did a little bowling. Indian society had become more complex with the addition of agriculture and temple mounds.

The Spanish, followed by the French, and later the English, were not interested in recording the Indians' lifestyles or opinions. Anthropology was to wait another 200 years to become a serious study. And long before that time European disease, war, whiskey, and slave hunts had all but destroyed the Indian culture. The Indians were friendly to the European explorers for many years, but, after being misused particularly by the Spanish and at times kidnapped and sold into slavery in the West Indies, the white settler became the enemy.

By 1662 only about 660 Indians were left in the area. Most of them moved elsewhere in 1712, but the Yemassee, of the Creek Confederacy, revolted in 1715 against English settlers most probably at the instigation of the Spanish in St. Augustine. Indians living on Hilton Head in 1685 asked the Scottish colony of Stuarts Town at Port Royal to defend them, for even they, the Indians, were at the mercy of the marauding Spanish.

Long since gone from here, the Indians left us a legacy of names. Calaobe — Indian name for deep spring — is the probable source for Calibogue. Coosawhatchie. Hatchie is the Indian word for creek and Kussah was a tribe. Indian Springs: located between villa complexes of Indian Springs and Mariners Point on Skull Creek in Hilton Head Plantation. The name Skull Creek is said to be a corruption of "skulk," which was applied to the waterway because Indians used to skulk along the creek in their attacks upon white settlers on the Island. Maps of the

18th century are marked with "ruins of an Indian fort" on Pinckney Island whose original owner, Colonel Alexander Mackay, was an Indian trader.

So the legend and lure of this fertile land reached the Spanish in the West Indies. And they came.

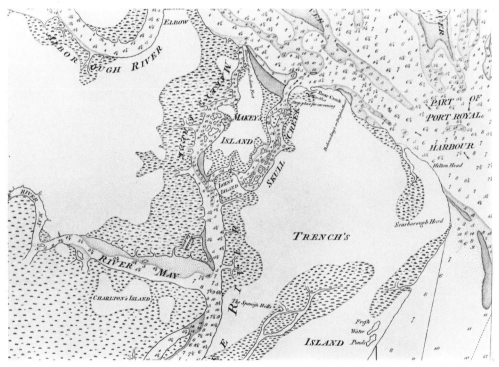

Detail of 1731 map. Note ruins of Indian Fort on Makey's Island (now Pinckney). On Hilton Head Island, note Golgotha, careening place, and fresh water ponds.

CHAPTER III

The First Europeans

Spain, under Ferdinand and Isabella, had won a vast empire abroad while in Europe their country was the number one power. Devout Roman Catholics themselves, the King and Queen determined through the terrors of the Inquisition that their religion would be supreme in all their domain and that only those who upheld Catholicism would be safe.

"As they passed Hilton Head Island, could they have paused at Spanish Wells to take on fresh water?"

Spanish settlers followed the charts of Columbus to an island in the West Indies which they named Hispaniola, the island that is now divided between Haiti and the Dominican Republic. The settlers enjoyed great wealth, but more manpower — meaning slaves — was needed for their sugar cane fields and cattle herds. The native Arawak tribes of Hispaniola had all but disappeared under the Spanish yoke. Disease and suicide finished them.

In 1521, a wealthy lawyer of the colonial capital of Santo Domingo, one Lucas Vasquez de Ayllón, sent out Francisco Gordillo to find the fabled "island of giants." In the northern Bahamas, Gordillo encountered his friend Pedro de Quexo who thought the trip sounded exciting. The two set off together in their respective caravels and in no time at all sighted land about where the present-day Santee River of South Carolina empties into the Atlantic Ocean. An Indian village was nearby and the adventurers spent some time trading with the friendly Indians, claiming and naming the territory Santa Elena, and impressing sixty unwilling natives on board the Spanish vessels for the return trip to Santo Domingo. On the way Gordillo's ship breathed its last and all on board were crowded onto De Quexo's.

Although the Indians were tall as legend and strong, most of the captives died quickly. De Allyón, the sponsor, took possession of a survivor who said he came from the land of Chicora. That sounded like a good name to De Allyón; so that's what he called his Indian. Judge Diego Columbus, son of Christopher, ordered the surviving Indians returned to their homeland, but De Allyón, good lawyer that he was, persuaded the judge to allow him to take Chicora to Spain and the court of Charles V to do a bit of showing off, possibly play a bit of personal politics, and gain a license for colonizing in the new land. The royal audience brought out the yarn spinner in Chicora, and he spun tales of magic balms to stretch the bones of royal children, of men with thick tails, and of a rich and fertile land.

De Allyón himself, swayed by the saga, was eager to see Santa Elena, but when he returned to Santo Domingo, he was slapped with a lawsuit by a man who claimed to have discovered the land first. But that didn't keep De Allyón from sending De Quexo out in 1525 to survey the unknown land. This time De Quexo sailed all the way to what we call the Chesapeake Bay.

In July, 1526, De Allyón finally set sail himself with six ships carrying some 500 people — families, horses, soldiers, priests, and the first black slaves. He sailed directly to the river where De Quexo first spotted land, put the travelers ashore, and Chicora, home at last, vanished into history. One wonders what tales he told around the campfires of his adventures.

The Spanish settlers continued looking for a more suitable site down the coast. As they passed Hilton Head Island, could they have paused at Spanish Wells to take on fresh water? Were the ships too heavily loaded and were a few horses put ashore?

The exact site that De Allyón selected for the first white settlement in the United States remains a mystery, but, as more evidence emerges, it is believed to have been off the coast of Georgia on St. Catherine's Island. The settlement was named San Miguel de Gualdape. Guale, a derivative of Gualdape, has long been an identifying Indian name for that coast as far north as Daufuskie Island. Hardship and privation depleted the colony. Three months after sailing from Santo Domingo on the adventure of his dreams, De Allyón died. Mutiny followed and the surviving 150 settlers sailed for home in the West Indies.

Discouraged by expeditions being swallowed up by this vast continent, King Charles V of Spain wanted no more than to claim the coast from Key West to the St. Lawrence as La Florida. Forty years would pass and only the threat of colonization by the French, along with their heretic Protestantism, would bring the Spanish back to these shores.

Spanish soliders capturing Indians on Santa Elena

CHAPTER IV
The French in Port Royal

All Europe was in religious turmoil in the middle of the 16th century. France was caught midway between Catholicism to the south, King Henry VIII's Church of England to the north and Martin Luther's spreading Protestantism to the east.

Catherine de Medici, as Queen Mother of France, kept the plot boiling between Roman Catholics and

"...the Frenchmen coaxed them with gifts, and the Indians signalled them to come ashore."

Protestants. Comte Gaspard de Coligny, Admiral of France, was the Protestant opposition leader and sought to establish colonies for religious freedom in the New World for his followers, the Huguenots. He chose Captain Jean Ribaut, a dedicated Huguenot who also had a chart of La Florida, to lead the expedition. Ribaut's lieutenant was Rene de Laudonniere to whom we are greatly indebted for his lengthy and descriptive account of the voyage.

On February 18, 1562, one hundred fifty military men set sail on a two-month voyage from France to Florida, then turned northward and landed near the mouth of the St. John's River. There, at a place he named Fort Caroline for his twelve-year-old King Charles IX, Jean Ribaut erected one of twenty heavy stone markers he was commissioned to place denoting France's claim to La Florida. The expedition did not linger, however, but sailed north past Georgia until it came to a "mightie river...which because of the fairnesse and largenesse thereof wee named Port Royall." From their ships they could see palm and fruit-bearing trees. The large island south of them, the one with the high bluffs, they named Ile de la Riviere Grande.

As nightfall approached, Ribaut's pilots advised him to bring his ships further up one of the rivers to avoid sudden storms. Indians hid or fled when they again saw white faces on big ships. After all, the last sailors had behaved rather badly toward them. Nevertheless, the Frenchmen coaxed them with gifts, and the Indians signalled them to come ashore.

Jean Ribaut had his men install another of France's stone pillars, bearing the royal arms, on one of the many islands of the Broad River. Some say it was Daws Island or even Pinckney Island. Others claim it was Bobb's Island, a small high-tide island near Dolphin Head in Hilton Head Plantation. Time and the mispronunciation of Spanish, French, English and Gullah could have corrupted Ribaut's Island into Bobb's Island as the word passed down through generations. The place Ribaut chose for a settlement, which was called Charlesfort, was near the present town of Port Royal and was the first Protestant settlement in the United States.

In short order Ribaut and his men (and their new Indian friends) built a fort, stocked it with food and munitions, and the Captain asked for volunteers to man the fort while he went back to France for more settlers. He was overwhelmed at the number who wished to remain behind and selected, some say, thirty. (Incidentally, Ribaut seems to have overlooked his commission to erect the remaining engraved stone markers. Perhaps, after establishing the colony and ships' supplies were low, he needed the heavy pillars for ballast.)

With a gun salute from Jean Ribaut's ships and an answering salvo from shore, the French captain sailed for home with the promise that he would return in six months. Instead, he found religious war, battle, and defeat when he reached France. He fled to England and the court of a fellow Protestant, Queen Elizabeth I. Ever mindful of expanding her empire, the astute Queen offered to finance Ribaut's return to his colony at Charlesfort. The loyal Frenchman, realizing a disadvantage to his country, tried to slip back to France but was captured and placed in the Tower of London.

Meanwhile, back at the little colony near Port Royal, the men had continued to win more friends among the Indians who helped them with food and building. But dissension and jealousy sprouted among the colonists, so much so that executions and mutiny followed. In the wake of the violence, Nicholas Barré was elected leader and, with the help of the Indians, they built a small ship to return to France. Rene de Laudonniere's account tells us that the men used resin from the pine trees and "a kind of mosse. . .to serve to calke the same." When the first ship built in the country to sail the ocean was complete, the homesick Frenchmen set sail with great joy — all but one. Young Guillaume Rouffi, of whom we shall hear more, decided to stay behind and marry the daughter of the Indian King Audusta. Lucky Rouffi. Was he clairvoyant? The voyage that began so joyously was beset by the worst tribulations.

When the Frenchmen were only one third of the way home, they were becalmed for three weeks. Food and water ran out. They ate their own shoes and leather jerkins and were compelled to cast lots for the one man who should die to sustain the others. Just as the men had reached the pit of despair, winds from the west, after so long a time, pushed the little vessel toward Europe. When land was in sight, the half-crazed survivors were picked up by an English barque. Those that were able were taken before Queen Elizabeth who, we know, had already heard about Charlesfort, and she placed the leader Barré in the Tower. It is Barré's map, believed to have been drawn while he was imprisoned, that locates the Charlesfort settlement. Did Barré meet Ribaut in the London Tower? If so, surely they had more to say than "small world."

Interest in La Florida was heating up not only in England but also in France and once again in Spain. Admiral de Coligny sent out another expedition with Laudonniere in command with an artist, Le Moyne, aboard. Le Moyne did almost all his sketches from tales told by sailors who had seen the Port Royal area. Laudonniere's group settled and began to build Fort Caroline on the St. John's River.

Almost simultaneously in 1563, Philip, now King of Spain, decided to take Charlesfort, not knowing the French had left Port Royal. Jean Ribaut had escaped at last from England and was sent out once again by his native France, this time to the new settlement at Fort Caroline. On the day that Ribaut reached his destination, the Spaniard Menéndez, with six hundred men (and a few women), arrived at Cape Canaveral and turned north to destroy the French.

CVm Galli in Floridam provinciam, secunda navigatione inftituta duce Laudonniero, appulif-
sent, ipse comitibus quinque & viginti pyxidarijs in continentem descendit, salute ab Indis ac-
cepta (nam catervatim ad eos conspiciendos advenerant) Rex Athoré quatuor aut quinq; mi-
liaribus à maris littore habitans etiam venit, & muneribus datis & acceptis, omnique humani-
tatis genere exhibito, indicavit se singulare quidpiam ipsis demonstrare velle, propterea orare ut
una proficiscerentur: adsentiuntur, quia tamen magno subditorum numero cinctum videbant, cautè & circumspe-
ctè cum eo profecti sunt. Jlle verò eos in insulam deduxit, in qua Ribaldus super tumulo quodam saxeum limitem
insignibus Regis Galliæ insculptum posuerat. Proximi facti, animadverterunt Indos hoc saxum non secus atque
idolum colere: nam ipse Rex eo salutato, & exhibito qualem à suis subditis accipere solet honore, osculo fixit, quem
imitati sunt ipsius subditi, ut idem faceremus adhortati. Ante saxum jacebant varia donaria fructibus ejus regio-
nis & radicibus edulibus, vel ad medicum usum utilibus constantia, vasáque plena odoratis oleis, arcus & sagittæ:
cinctum etiam erat, ab imo ad summum, florum omnis generis corollis, & arborum apud ipsos selectissimarum ra-
mis. Perspecto miserorum horum barbarorum ritu, ad suos redierunt observaturi commodissimun ad propugnacu-
lum extruendum locum. Est verò hic Rex Athoré formosus admodum, prudens, honestus, robustus & procera admodum statura, nostrorum hominu maximos sesquipeda superans, modesta quadam gravitate præditus, ut in eo ma-
jestas spectabilis reluceat. Cum matre matrimonium contraxit, & ex ea plures liberos utriusq; sexus suscepit, quos
percusso fœmore nobis ostendit: postquam verò ipsi desponsata fuit, parens ejus Saturioua illam amplius non attigit.

B 3

*DeBry engraving of LeMoyne drawing. Athore shows Laudonniere the
Marker Column set up by Ribaut.*

11

CHAPTER V
Spain Again

Traffic was heavy between La Florida and France and Spain as well as Havana. Hernando Manrique de Rojas set out with orders to destroy the fort and garrison at Charlesfort; Laudonnière was sailing for the St. John's River; Ribaut was right behind him with reinforcements; and Menéndez, as we have seen, arrived with overpowering odds to nip the new French Florida settlement in the bud.

"A mature Queen Elizabeth. . . .was ready for the English to become sole occupants of this fertile land."

Rojas accomplished his assignment in Port Royal without bloodshed, having fired the abandoned Charlesfort and encountering the aforementioned Guillaume Rouffi, son-in-law to the Indian king. The adaptable Rouffi exchanged his Indian clothes for a Spanish doublet and led the latest in a line of tourists to the stone marker erected by Ribaut. Swords are persuasive instruments and it is even possible that, in order to save his life, Guillaume not only changed his name to the Spanish Guillermo Rufín but also quickly converted from Protestant to Catholic. We know that he returned to Havana and then Spain, having been impressed into Spanish service. Rojas also took along the French stone pillar, which the Indians were worshipping, as a sign of mission accomplished.

Jean Ribaut reached Fort Caroline, his destination and his destiny. Pedro Menéndez de Avilés landed with Spanish standards flying just south of Fort Caroline at a place he called St. Augustine. In a series of bloody encounters Menéndez destroyed all but a few Frenchmen who escaped by boat, the writer Laudonnière and the artist Le Moyne among them. Jean Ribaut was captured and executed.

Spain was once again all powerful in La Florida. Early in 1566 Menéndez, assured that St. Augustine was established, took a small fleet north along the coast of Guale (Georgia) and entered Port Royal Sound. He sailed past Hilton Head which the Spanish called Isla de los Osos (Island of Bears) and the remains of Charlesfort, landing on Parris Island where he built a fort, the first structure of Santa Elena, which he determined to make the capital of all the East Coast which Spain claimed. In July another group of men arrived from Spain — 250 in all — to build a number of houses. In this group, as guide and interpreter, was the French-Indian-Spanish Guillermo Rufin who, by this time, had accumulated quite a few frequent traveler credits.

While Santa Elena acquired more buildings, explorers went westward. After two years, the adventurers returned saying the land was "good for bread and wine and all kinds of livestock" which helped bring many more settlers to Santa Elena. By 1569 the colony numbered 327. Jesuit missionaries were spreading the Word among the Indians. Menéndez himself returned in 1571 with his wife and elaborate home furnishings, including a canopied bed. He and his friends dressed finely when they attended the simple church. Apparently he did not remain long in the capital city of Santa Elena for he died three years later in Spain.

Because of years of misdeeds among their Indian neighbors, antagonisms grew and finally exploded in 1576 when Guale Indians killed a chief who had been baptized by Spanish priests. Reprisals and revenge ravaged the entire coast, and the thriving town of Santa Elena was not spared.

The Orista Indians, living close to Santa Elena, attacked, killing and burning in and around the town. Survivors raced for the boats. As the townspeople set off for St. Augustine, they saw ten years of hard labor burning before their eyes. Again the King of Spain would not give up. By 1580 the Indian uprising was quelled, and Santa Elena was re-built with 60 houses and a new fort.

In Europe, however, the scales of power were tipping toward England. A mature Queen Elizabeth, who had listened twenty years earlier to both Ribaut and Laudonnière tell of the wonders of the Carolina coast, was ready for the English to become sole occupants of this fertile land. In 1586 she sent Sir Frances Drake with 42 vessels and 2,000 men to chase the Spanish from La Florida. As Drake attacked first Santo Domingo, then Cartagena and St. Augustine (where the defenders fled into the woods), the 33 families at Santa Elena were ordered to abandon the town and concentrate all remaining Spaniards in St. Augustine.

Recently, in 1985, after six seasons of digging on the golf course of the Parris Island Marine Corps Base, Archaeologist Stanley South uncovered two of the forts, a small plaza bordered by houses, and the remains of a vineyard revealing the location of Santa Elena, the long-lost capital of Spain's La Florida.

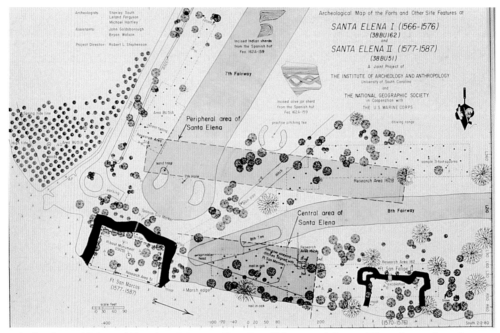

Archeological Map of Fort San Marcos, Fort San Felipe, and Santa Elena located on the present site of the Parris Island golf course.

CHAPTER VI
The English Come to Stay

*E*ngland expanded to this hemisphere primarily to produce staple crops that were unavailable in the British Isles. Spain had been searching for both precious metals and slaves. France needed freedom of worship by the followers of Martin Luther. Although Sir Frances Drake cleared the decks, so to speak, Queen Elizabeth was not to see the settlement

"...Captain William Hilton, on his ship ADVENTURE, sailed on exploration of the area from Barbados..."

of the Port Royal area by the English during her reign. Another half century passed with a Catholic Queen Mary who was followed by a commoner, each creating enough turmoil at home to prevent expansion abroad.

King Charles II, in 1663, granted the coast to eight Lords Proprietors and they, in turn, named their acquisition Carolina to honor the donor. These proprietors were: The Earl of Clarendon, the Duke of Albemarle, Lord Craven, Lord Berkeley, Lord Ashley, Sir George Carteret, Sir William Berkeley, and Sir John Colleton. Today, throughout South Carolina, rivers, streets, towns and counties bear their name.

In August of that same year Captain William Hilton, on his ship *Adventure*, sailed on exploration of the area from Barbados and rescued a party of shipwrecked Englishmen (as an unexpected bonus) who told horror stories of the Indians.

Captain Hilton's log records that when his ship was about 28 miles north of Port Royal in St. Helena's Sound, Indians came boldly aboard, using Spanish terms and showing familiarity with firearms. In this way the English heard of their shipwrecked fellow countrymen who were encamped with the Indians. When, after many promises and strange actions, the Indians did not deliver the

A
RELATION

OF

A Discovery lately made on the Coast of
FLORIDA,

(From Lat. 31. to 33 Deg. 45 Min. North-Lat.)

By *William Hilton* Commander, and
Commissioner with Capt *Anthony Long,*
and *Peter Fabian*, in the Ship *Adventure*, which
set Sayl from *Spikes* Bay, *Aug.* 10. 1663. and was
set forth by several Gentlemen and Mer-
chants of the Island of *BARBADOES.*

Giving an account of the nature and tempera-
ture of the Soyl, the manners and disposition
of the Natives, and whatsoever else is
remarkable therein.

Together with

Proposals made by the Commissioners
of the Lords Proprietors, to all such per-
sons as shall become the first Setlers on the
Rivers, Harbors, and Creeks there.

LONDON,
Printed by *J. C.* for *Richard Moon*, Book-seller in
Bristol, 1664.

Title page from 1664 record by William Hilton

Englishmen, Hilton became worried and suspicious, believing Spaniards to be lurking on land. William Hilton personally went ashore at the abandoned and burned Spanish settlement of Santa Elena and recorded seeing a timbered Great House with a Cross before it. An English captive was brought on board — but there were more. While continuing to negotiate with the Indians and taking soundings of the waters hereabouts, Hilton approached Port Royal Sound by an inland waterway. He then decided to approach the huge sound from the sea. It was then that he sighted the high bluffs of the island which he named for himself — Hilton Head Island.

For almost a week Captain William Hilton cruised along the shore and made note of all he saw. Of the land he saw in the Port Royal area and a little to the north, he wrote, "Now our understanding of the land of Port Royal, River Jordan, River Grandie or Edistow is as followeth: the lands are laden with large tall oaks, walnut and bayes, except, facing the sea, it is most pines tall and good. The land generally, except where the pines grow, is a good soyl, covered with black mold, in some places, a foot, in some places half a foot, and in other places lesse, with clay underneath mixed with sand; and we think may produce any thing as well as most part of the Indies that we have seen. The Indians plant in the worst land because they cannot cut down the timber in the best, and yet have plenty of corn, pompions, water-mellons, musk-mellons. Although the land be over grown with weeds through their lasinesse, yet they have two or three crops of corn a year, as the Indians themselves inform us. The countrey abounds with grapes, large figs and peaches; the woods with deer, conies, turkeys, quails, curlues, plovers, teile, herons; and as the Indians say, in winter with swans, geese, cranes, duck and mallard and innumerable of other water-fowls whose names we know not, which lie in the rivers, marshes, and on the sands; oysters in abundance, with great store of mussels; a sort of fair crabs, and a round shellfish called horsefeet. The rivers stored plentifully with fish that we saw play and leap.

"There are great marshes, but most as far as we saw little worth, except for a root that grows in them the Indians make good bread of.

"The land, we suppose, is healthful; the English that were cast away on that coast in July were there most part of that time of year that is sickly in Virginia; and notwithstanding hard usage, and lying on the ground naked, yet had their perfect healths all the time. The natives are very healthful; we saw many very

17

aged amongst them. The ayr is clear and sweet, the countrey very pleasant and delightful. And we could wish that all they that want a happy settlement, of our English nation, were well transported thither."

So much for the complaining, shipwrecked English who said the Indians treated them cruelly. Captain Hilton, although he did not tarry for fear of the Indians, not only named Hilton Head Island but was undoubtedly the Island's first public relations man. The final sentence of his report has been repeatedly quoted in book, brochures, and articles.

When Hilton's report was read back in England, this perhaps sounded too good to be true; so the Lords Proprietors, in 1666, sent their secretary, Robert Sandford, to verify Hilton's findings. He, too, found friendly Indians with a Great House and a bowling 'plaine' for recreation, but Sandford opted for Edisto Island, no doubt·because it was further from the Spanish in St. Augustine. Along with Sandford came a 20-year-old surgeon, Dr. Henry Woodward, who was curious about Hilton Head Island and stayed when the others sailed on. A surgeon at that time was really a barber who had added "bleeding and bone setting" to his skills. Woodward found a friend in the Indian, Shadoo, who had been taken back to Barbados by Hilton and treated well. Robert Sandford recorded, "The Cassique (chief) placed Woodward upon the throne and after led him forth and shewed him a large field of Maiz which hee told him should bee his." The knowledge Dr. Henry Woodward acquired of Indian language and his establishment of trust with the Indians counted for much as English settlers made homes in Port Royal and as far north as Charleston. More should be said about this young man to whom so little recognition has been given.

Dr. Woodward's life reads like a swashbuckler novel. He continued to live with the Indians until the Spanish captured him and imprisoned him in St. Augustine where the buccaneer Robert Serle freed Woodward in a raid in 1669 and sailed away, only to be shipwrecked in a hurricane off the island of Nevis where Woodward was cast shore. A year later, another English expedition stopped at Nevis and took Dr. Woodward aboard and directly back to Hilton Head. About that time a fierce tribe of Westoes swarmed into Port Royal and almost obliterated the peaceful Cusabo Indians.

When English colonists actually came for serious settlement, the frightened Cusabo were hiding so deeply that it was two days before the Indians learned

A 1778 Plan of De Port Royal and D'awfoskee

of the ships' arrival. Because of the warring Westoes, both Indians and English agreed that north of Port Royal was safer for settling; so, in 1670, they were off to the Ashley River and Charles Town. Two other factors played a part in the choice of place: further inland provided much more protection from hurricanes and from the marauding pirates which plagued the coast. As for the Spanish, they had signed a treaty in Madrid that any settled English town in North America would not be molested.

In 1684 the Scots under Lord Cardross came to the Port Royal area, but about four years later the Spanish, ignoring their treaty, came again and burned the Scots' settlement. The plan was to move against Charles Town further north but a hurricane prevented the attack.

One method of encouraging the English of the West Indies to settle in Carolina was to give anyone 500 acres of land if he invested 1,000 pounds of sugar in the settlement. The land around Port Royal was claimed in this way. Plantings were brought from Barbados: sugar cane, indigo, ginger, sesame, citrus trees, and cotton. Indians contributed corn, beans, and potatoes. The colonists, because of native mulberry trees, tried the silk industry but found that felling trees for shipbuilding and repair was quicker and more profitable. Cattle and pigs thrived on the islands. Surrounded by water, no fences were necessary.

Large tracts of land were called baronies. The Hilton Head part of a barony was granted, on August 16, 1698, to John Bayley of Ballingclough, County of Tipperary, Kingdom of Ireland, and the first English development of the Island was begun. But before successful settlement could take place, there was trouble with the Indians. Using Spanish encouragement and headquarters in St. Augustine, the Yemasees struck in a surprise uprising that would have been a blood bath for the Beaufort area settlers had not one injured man reached an outlying farm to sound the alarm for escape. Armed and sponsored by the tireless Spanish, the war with the Yemasees went on until 1728 when the Indians were chased back to St. Augustine — those that were alive — from Bloody Point on Daufuskie Island.

Prior to 1715 the Yemasees had been friendly, allying themselves with the colonists to offset raids against the Yemasees by the North Carolina Tuscaroras. Colonel John Barnwell got his nickname, "Tuscarora Jack," from campaigns he led against the Tuscaroras in 1711 and 1712. For these and other acts of bravery

Barnwell was granted 1,000 acres on the northwest corner of Hilton Head Island by the Lords Proprietors in 1717 and became the Island's first white settler. Colonel Alexander Mackey, Indian trader, bought the island now known as Pinckney, but, for Hilton Head Island, sales were slow. Another John Bayley, son of the Ballingclough Bayley, appointed Alexander Trench as the Island's first real estate agent. Unsuccessful at sales, Trench used Hilton Head for cattle grazing, and the Island became known on maps as Trench's Island as late as the Revolutionary War although sales and settlement were to come long before then.

Trench did sell some land in June, 1729, to John Gascoigne which Gascoigne called John's Island after himself. Later Gascoigne's purchase became known as Jenkin's Island for another owner. Today the land, which is joined to Hilton Head by a dirt causeway that hardly anyone notices, is known as Windmill Harbour.

Throughout Carolina the Anglican Episcopal Church was the official religion. Church parishes were official districts and remained so until the end of the nineteenth century. Hilton Head Island was part of St. Luke's Parish. A semblance of order was being established, and it appeared that the threat of both Spanish and Indians had vanished and beautiful Hilton Head was at last safe for settlement.

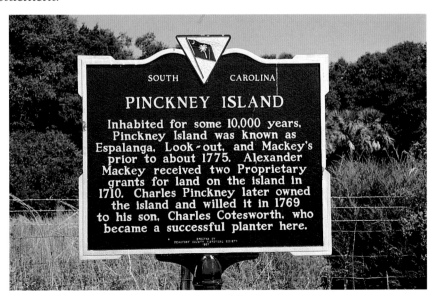

Historical marker at entrance to Pinckney Island

CHAPTER VII
The Planters

Considering the glowing reports that were to follow years later, it is hard to imagine the negative reaction of one James Sutherland, writing of his coastal voyage about 1730. Of Beaufort, Port Royal, and "Hill Town head," he wrote, "where are but a few Stragling houses meanly inhabited, which on the Contrary ought always to have a great many Men to prevent

"...in 1888, another Henry Talbird, a member of the clergy, wrote of an oak which stands today and is known as the Talbird oak."

the Pyrates destroying the Country. Here is a very good Harbour but difficult to come into, because of several Sand banks, & is the Southermost Settlement belonging to the English except Hill Town head, where are Fish in abundance but very few inhabitants, The People being afraid to settle there, so near the Spaniards of St. Augustin's who are continually encouraging the Indians to destroy them, which makes the croud to the Northward to be under the protection of the Northern Colonies. This part as indeed the whole Country is well stored with all Manner of Cattle and Timber fit for Masts Yards &ca. for Ships of Six Hundred Tonn and upwards." (*South Carolina Historical Magazine*, April 1967).

A newspaper ad in Charleston, 1733, was more encouraging. "For sale: Hog Island (now Blue Heron Point)...residence...orange, apple, peach, nectarine, and plum trees..." By 1766, twenty-five families were living on Hilton Head Island, planting, building homes, and debating whether to revolt against the Mother Country.

When the Revolution actually came ten years later, the Island was filled with staunch supporters of the Cause, and the island immediately south — Daufuskie — was occupied by Tory families loyal to the Crown. British warships could be sighted off Savannah and Charleston. Naturally a fertile and almost undefended

A 1939 painting of Hilton Head Island

Hilton Head Island was a target for foraging and raiding British aided by planters from Daufuskie Island.

Charleston fell to the British in 1780. Lieutenant John Talbird, whose home was on Skull Creek, was captured at that time. The Revolutionary War continued for weeks on Hilton Head and Daufuskie after Cornwallis' surrender at Yorktown on October 19, 1781. On the day of the surrender, Mary Ann Talbird (the captured John's wife) looked out toward Skull Creek to see a landing party of British soldiers led by Isaac Martinangele of Daufuskie. Now, Isaac's wife was Mary Ann Talbird's sister, and for this reason Isaac Martinangele ordered the soldiers to remove all the house furnishings and place them beneath a large oak tree before burning the Talbird residence to the ground and departing for more undefended sites. Later that day terrified attendants, with eyes glancing back toward the creek, awaited Mrs. Talbird as she gave birth to a son whom she named Henry, but, because of the historic day on which he was born, was known throughout his life as "Yorktown Henry."

More than a century later, in 1888, another Henry Talbird, a member of the clergy, wrote of an oak which stands today and is known as the Talbird oak. Perhaps it was the same oak which sheltered the possessions of Mary Ann Talbird. The Reverend Talbird wrote from his residence in Florida, "The tree used to be my playground in my boyhood."

The Revolutionary War was not over on Hilton Head. A few nights after the Talbird torching, word came that another raid was planned, and plantation owners saddled their horses to thwart the landing party from Daufuskie. Their effort was futile. Just before dawn Hilton Head planters Charles Davant and John Andrews, riding ahead of the others, saw movement among the broad oaks near the crossroads now called Folly Field and William Hilton Parkway. A shot rang out from the shadows. Charles Davant slumped in his saddle. Andrews galloped back to the others, and Davant's horse, with his wounded master, raced for home where Davant died after he gasped the name of Martinangele as his assailant. Revenge was not long in coming. A band of men who called themselves the Bloody Legion raided and plundered the residences on Daufuskie Island and executed Martinangele, the Tory.

The two Revolutionary War events cited above are the most written about concerning Hilton Head Island; however, it should be noted that, during the War, the British burned every plantation house on Skull Creek and carried off any captured slaves to be sold in the West Indies.

Savannah fell in 1778 because a plucky British colonel found a secret but swampy passage around the defenders and attacked the city from the waterways. In almost a rehearsal for Sherman's march to the sea 100 years later, British General Augustine Prevost and his 6,000 Redcoats were joined by runaway slaves and a few Indians, plundering and burning unguarded plantations up to 35 miles inland from Hilton Head. At Coosawatchie's Tullifinny River Bridge, Lieutenant John Laurens, with only 100 volunteers, made a stand against the overwhelming British forces. When Laurens received support from General Benjamin Lincoln, the British were eventually driven back toword Savannah. During the seesaw battle many more slaves were captured by the Redcoats, cruelly treated and either left to die of disease or become slaves once again in the West Indies.

Historical marker at intersection of Highway 278 and Folly Field Road

CHAPTER VIII
The Golden Age

The Revolutionary War brought considerable hardships to the planters, but now landowners on Hilton Head Island were free at last from war and the King. Within ten years, an incredible recovery had been made. In 1790, William Elliott II of Myrtle Bank Plantation (near Dolphin Head in Hilton Head Plantation) grew the first successful crop of long-staple cotton, the famous Sea Island cotton, which would bring great riches to the planters and usher in a Golden Age.

Learning a more positive attitude toward marketing land from the failure of Alexander Trench, another sales agent, Peter Bayley (heir to John Bayley who had hired Trench), ran an advertisement in 1784 that noted for sale "those

"By 1834 riches and travel brought silver chalices to the Zion Chapel of Ease."

famed, healthy and pleasantly located indigo lands on Scull (note the change in spelling) Creek." Yet another Bayley, Benjamin, set up sales offices in Charleston. Hilton Head real estate sales were brisk. The names Pope, Baynard, Elliott, Graham, and Stoney were prominent. Hilton Head was finally off and running. The births of Island babies were announced with regularity in Charleston newspapers.

For in-depth lineage and ownerships of ante-bellum plantations, the Reverend Robert E. H. Peeples' concise book, *Tales of Ante Bellum Hilton Head Island Families*, is the authority. A cat's cradle of marriage and intermarriage, the book is full of double first cousins and a handbook on how to keep land within the family circle. Twenty-five families planted Hilton Head's 25,000 acres while by 1808 Edisto Island's 28,811 acres was home to 236 white citizens and 2,609 slaves with the land almost entirely planted out. Comparatively speaking, hunting and fishing would have supplied Hilton Head Islanders with great abundance.

William Elliott II's success with cotton was a direct result of his selecting the best seeds from the best pods of the best plants and saving those seeds for the following year's crop, assuring the continued improvement of the product. This very important point escaped the Union forces in 1861. They quickly shipped ALL the cotton north without reserving the best seed.

A neighboring planter, William Seabrook, who owned four plantations on Scull Creek, used marsh muck to fertilize his cotton and, on alternate years, ground oyster shells. When his crop yields soared, other planters followed his example.

Before cotton, indigo was tried and rice was grown on plantations which were safe from salt water intrusion which would ruin young rice seedlings. Any other crops were for the sole use of planters, their families and their slaves.

Houses on the Island in the prosperous period between the Revolutionary and Civil Wars were not the pillared mansions of romantic novels. Although large and airy, the majority were not the owners' main house. Lavish town houses were kept in Beaufort or Savannah or even Charleston. Charles Cotesworth Pinckney, who owned nearby Pinckney Island, married the daughter of creator of Sea Island cotton, William Elliott II. The Honorable Mr. Pinckney remembered his grand-mother Elliott's house at Myrtle Bank as follows: 'I recall an old-fashioned country home on the river bank, when the shades of evening and breath of spring lured the family to the piazza. The harp in hands of a skillful musician, accompanied by her brothers on flute and clarinet, imprinted sweet sounds on the memory. . .Down the broad avenue over-arched by the patriarchal live oaks and verdant magnolia, you saw the moonbeams dancing on the waters of Port Royal, the peerless river of our southern coast, while the orange trees and jasmine em-bowering the piazza and climbing up its posts perfumed the air with odors sweet. . .The Negroes' keen ear for music would draw them from their homes. Seated on the grass around the house, they counted it a privilege to hear Miss Mary's harp.

During the Union occupation, one of the New England teachers wrote of the Widow Stoney's house which he and others occupied. 'The plantation houses are built of hard pine, which is handsome on the floors, but the rest of the wood-work is painted. . .The walls are always left white. . .clapboards are unknown, but hard-pineboards a foot or more wide are put on in the same manner and everything outside is whitewashed. . .very attractive-looking, with grapevines and honeysuckle, and pinewoods near. . .The (slave) quarters are a fourth of a mile or so from the house and a praise house (a small place of worship) stands near them."

Chasing the Devil Fish in South Carolina

By 1788 the planters felt a need for their own place of worship, and a small Episcopal Church — Zion Chapel of Ease — was built. All that remains today is its cemetery, which opened its first grave in 1795, at the headwaters of Broad Creek. Next to the church was a Muster House and also a Masonic Lodge. All the buildings were of wood and after the Civil War, they "just walked away," to use the term favored by Island natives, meaning that board by board the buildings were put to other uses. For a time the crossroads of Folly Field and Mathews Drive were the center of community activity on Hilton Head. By 1834 riches and travel brought silver chalices to the Zion Chapel of Ease. The chalices were made by Barnard silversmiths in Paternoster Row, London. Services were held in the

Chapel about half a dozen times each year because of the great distance vicars were compelled to travel from one Episcopal church to another.

The story of those silver chalices is truly a saga. During the occupation of Hilton Head by Union forces, both the chalices disappeared. In 1920, the family of a young bride in Philadelphia was searching for old silver goblets to adorn the bride's first home. Finding two old "goblets," tarnished with age, the parents brought them home from the antique dealer, polished them, and were astonished to read from the engraving that the chalices belonged to a church on Hilton Head Island. Of course at that time the closest Episcopal Church of full orders was in Beaufort. The considerate Philadelphia couple returned the chalices to Beaufort with the stipulation that, if ever again there was an Episcopal Church on Hilton Head Island, the chalices would go back "home."

About the time that Zion Chapel of Ease was built, John Hanahan began accumulating land, and as the years moved along, his 1,000 acres became known as Honey Horn. Say Hanahan aloud several times, and it sounds reasonable that it shoud become Honey Horn. Other planters, such as James and John Stoney owned the 770-acre Otterburn (now corrupted to Otter Hole).

Just south of the Lawtons' Calibogia Plantation was the 1,000-acre Braddock's Point Plantation, named for Daniel Cutler Braddock, captain of the Scout Boat maintained as a lookout against the Spaniards from St. Augustine from 1740 until the 1763 Treaty of Paris. Then Captain Jack Stoney became the owner of the plantation. Now Captain Jack, during the Revolutionary War, was licensed to pirate against British ships moving out of Savannah up the coast. He would strike for the last ship in a convoy and quickly disappear with his prize up Calibogue Sound into Broad Creek. The cargo was then transferred at night to Beaufort or Charleston through the maze of waterways while British gunboats searched in vain. With his winnings, Captain Jack Stoney built the tabby mansion we now know as the Stoney-Baynard Ruins (Sea Pines Plantation) in 1793.

The story goes that William Eddings Baynard, around 1840, won the plantation in a high-stake poker game in a Bluffton house which has since been called the Card House. Baynard also purchased the Davenport house in Savannah for his town house and built the impressive Baynard Mausoleum in the churchyard of Zion Chapel of Ease. He ultimately inherited both Muddy Creek and Spanish Wells plantations. The Baynard family possessed the flamboyance attributed to all Southern planters by writers of historical fiction. William Baynard's grand-daughter eloped from the second-story window of the same Card House. Another relative, a millionaire planter of Edisto Island and born in 1796, in his mid-fifties (considered quite old in those days) impressed the ladies by racing his elegant matched horses and shining rig around the Lawtonville Baptist Church during services — a great disturbance when the heat required the broad windows to be kept open. In 1864 the same "racy" Baynard saved the College of Charleston from extinction near the end of the Civil War with a gift of $166,000 for its endowment, the principal of which remains intact today.

The master of the Baynard mansion in Braddock's Point Plantation died in his prime, only 49 years old. His wife, Catherine Adelaide, was only 42 when she died five years later in 1854. They were both laid to rest behind the carved doors of the Baynard mausoleum in Zion Cemetery, undisturbed until vandals during the World War II years broke down the magnificent marble doors to the mausoleum, opened the iron caskets and threw the caskets into the nearby marsh.

Miniature of Squire William Pope of Hilton Head Island, born 1788, died 1862

Portraits of these hard-working (and playing) planters, and their letters and diaries prove that they were unusually intelligent, educated, and civilized people. They established a level of society heretofore unattained in the new United States. In spite of his elegance and education, Squire William Pope, the largest landowner on the Island during its Golden Age, wrote that he had attended the funeral of his friend Barnard when he should have written Baynard. Small wonder that, if a man of Squire Pope's achievements could misspell a friend's name, we have changed and changed again the names of places and people on maps and in our speech.

The pursuit of happiness (and wealth) was interrupted on August 22, 1813, when the British once again landed on undefended Hilton Head Island and burned most of the houses near deep water.

The Zion cemetery, located at the intersection of Folly Field Road and Highway 278.

Cast-iron coffin from the Baynard mausoleum in the Zion Cemetery.

With Island economy booming, the planters rebuilt and were able to pursue other high goals in the bigger picture. Revolutionary War General Charles Cotesworth Pinckney, who owned the nearby island named for him, had been a member of the Constitutional Convention and was later Minister to France. He was twice a presidential candidate, at different times Secretary of War and of State, and declined George Washington's appointment to the Supreme Court. Although there were three plantations on Pinckney Island — Old Place, Crescent, and The Point — Charles Cotesworth Pinckney did not see his holdings until 1818 when he traveled there to prepare for President James Monroe's overnight visit to Pinckney Island on his way from Beaufort to Savannah when the President toured the South.

Tabby ruins located at the intersection of Squire Pope Road and Gum Tree Road.

William Elliott III, son of the long-staple cotton grower at Myrtle Bank, continued planting, but also attained a great deal of fame as a sportsman and writer as well as serving in the United States Senate. His 1859 writings about devil-fishing with harpoons in Port Royal Sound are still quoted. We suppose, from his description, that the devil-fish was the dread ray. The fish's body oils and flesh were used as fertilizer. Elliott would sail over from Bay Point near his Beaufort home, fish, and land to inspect his cotton fields. (At low tide, in Port Royal Sound near Dolphin Head, may be seen the foundation of the Elliott house.) Of one fishing excursion, Elliott wrote, "The fish measured 16 feet across, which I suppose to be the medium size of those that visit our waters..."

In the South it was a time of great riches and abundance. South Carolina was among the richest of the states, and Hilton Head Island produced several of its millionaires. Author and statesman William John Grayson recollects his youth. "During my boyhood, many men of the Revolution were still alive. They were a jovial and somewhat rough race, liberal, social, warm-hearted, hospitable, addicted to deep drinking, hard-swearing, and practical joking and not a little given to loose language and indelicate allusions...They were fond of dinners, barbecues and hunting clubs. The abundance of deer in the country led to associations for sport in every neighborhood. They met monthly or oftener to hunt and dine. Afterwards when deer became less numerous, the club assembled to eat, drink and talk of politics and planting. At these festivals no man was permitted to go home sober."

Heated discussions and attempts to preserve their way of life sowed the seed of another revolution, this time a revolt against their own government, a civil war, brother against brother — a war that was to devastate the South, destroy a Golden Age, and leave prostrate a land that, in the Port Royal area alone, produced three million dollars worth of cotton in a single year.

Historical marker at entrance to
Pinckney Island

Historical Marker at Zion Cemetery

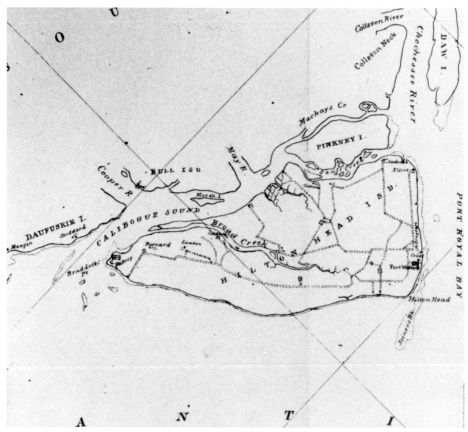

1861 U.S. Coast Survey map shows forts and locations of plantation houses.

CHAPTER IX
The Civil War

South Carolina, as a rule, has been either first or last in almost everything — no middle ground for the Palmetto State. She was the first to secede from the United States and several places claim the Secessionist Oak where the plan was plotted. The firing upon the Federal Fort in Charleston harbor by the newly formed Confederacy in April, 1861, marked the beginning of four years of a War Between the States as Southerners still call the strife. Others born below the Mason-Dixon Line would keep the cause alive after more than 100 years by calling the war 'The Late Unpleasantness', or 'The War of Yankee Aggression.'

". . . and Hilton Head's Fort Walker received bow guns and another broadside, a tactic repeated until the forts surrendered."

South Carolina declared itself a free and independent state in December, 1860, and on January 1, 1861, Fort Walker was begun on Hilton Head Island. The coasts of South Carolina, Georgia, and East Florida were declared a military department, and General Robert E. Lee was assigned to command.

The War Department in Washington realized the strategic importance of Port Royal Sound. Savannah and Charleston were two of the most important cities in the South, and the area surrounding Port Royal was the richest. 40,000 people, 83% of them slaves, lived in the Port Royal area. Taking the poorly manned Hilton Head Island and Bay Point across Port Royal Sound would be an easy task for a naval assault. Troops could then cut the Charleston-Savannah Railroad and bring the South to her knees in short order.

On October 29, 1861, 77 vessels sailed from Hampton Roads, Virgina, under the command of Commodore Samuel F. du Point from his flagship *Wabash*, a steam frigate which carried 11-inch cannon. (Commodore du Pont knew the Port

Royal area well, for he had spent many summers as a guest at Grahamville, a favorite resort of Southern planters.) The Federal assault fleet moved toward its Port Royal destination carrying 13,000 troups, 1,500 horses, 500 surf boats, and 1,000 laborers to build a town and fortresses to blockade the South and supply the troups which would do battle on land. General Thomas West Sherman commanded the troups. (This General Sherman should not be confused with General William Tecumseh Sherman who would later torch the South as he marched.)

One of history's most disastrous hurricanes scattered the fleet off Cape Hatteras with four ships lost. After the storm, each captain set his own course and rendezvoused outside the entrance to Port Royal Sound. A sounding operation by seven of the vessels was attacked by Flag Officer Josiah Tattnall, a veteran of the United States Navy now upholding the Confederacy of his native Georgia, and his little fleet which consisted of Tattnall's flagship (a river steamer) and three converted tugboats. The following day, November 6, Tattnall's navy attacked again but was about as effective as gnats on a raging boar.

The 3,000 defenders at Fort Walker and Fort Beauregard at Bay Point were forewarned of the Union fleet's arrival, both as to time and strength. A Southern woman who was on intimate terms with a member of President Lincoln's cabinet had notified Confederate President Jefferson Davis of the plan. Although there were guns at a fort on the south end of Hilton Head at Braddock's Point, they were not manned. All available men had been rushed to Fort Walker.

On November 7, in an elliptical attack, the United States armada circled the wide Port Royal Sound, firing on each fort as it passed. Fort Beauregard received the broadsides, and Hilton Head's Fort Walker received bow guns and another broadside, a tactic repeated until the forts surrendered. The flagship *Wabash*, within four hours, launched 888 beautifully accurate shells. The gunboat *Pocahontas*, commanded by Percival Drayton, enfiladed fire that damaged Fort Walker seriously. By noon the defending Confederates knew the battle was lost and that they must evacuate before the assaulting troops stormed ashore from surf boats. 12,653 Federal troops landed, having lost only eight dead and 23 wounded. For the Confederacy, 59 were killed or wounded.

The encounter was reported in an eyewitness account by General Egbert L. Viele, second in command to General Sherman. "The two works to be encountered, Forts Walker and Beauregard, situated on either side of the harbor,

Pier 1,300 feet long. View of wharf from top of signal station

Port Royal House

View of Courtyard of Provost Marshall and Guard House. A battalion of Dahoney Soldiery on duty guarding Rebel prisoners

were in themselves models in their construction, admirably designed, well mounted with guns of heavy caliber and manned by as gallant a set of men as ever fought for any cause or country. They were well drilled and disciplined and were all sanguine of victory. A telegram from Jefferson Davis had given them the true destination of the fleet; they knew its power to a ship and its strength to a man. Notwithstanding all this they prepared to meet the odds that were pitted against them with calm determination. The manner in which they served their guns to the last while a hurricane of shot and shell poured in upon them elicited the unqualified admiration of every soldier and sailor. . .One of the sad incidents of this engagement was the fact that while General T. F. Drayton of Charleston, South Carolina, commanded the forces at Fort Walker, his brother, Captain Percival Drayton, also a South Carolinian, was the commander of the *Pocahontas* one of the Union vessels in the attack. General Drayton's residence at Hilton Head was riddled with shells, some of them in all probability coming from Captain Drayton's vessel. This was truly a fratricidal combat."

Not only was the Drayton family sundered, but also the du Ponts. Samuel Francis du Pont who commanded the assault on Port Royal and his kinsman Charles E. du Pont and his wife Julia Kirk du Pont refugeed from Beaufort to Grahamville. They are buried there.

Bombardment from the Union fleet was so awesome and overwhelming that the Confederates fled, leaving their flags flying and tents standing with all supplies. The Confederate mosquito fleet scurried up Skull Creek to Ferry Point where they participated in transporting the retreating Southern defenders to the mainland and Bluffton where General Drayton again assumed command. With an obvious rout in progress and with overpowering odds in their favor, the question arises, "Why did not the Union forces press their advantage, pursue and press on to Charleston or Savannah?" A council of war was held immediately upon landing at Fort Walker, and only one officer in command favored pushing onward. Even today, once our beaches are reached, Northern visitors are loath to leave these shores. During the next three years, nine attempts were made to cut the Charleston-Savannah Railroad but it was January, 1865, after Pocotaligo was abandoned by the Confederates, that the Union forces succeeded in taking the railroad.

Map showing the Savannah, Georgia, to Charleston, South Carolina Railroad

Plaque commemorating General Thomas Fenwick Drayton and his brother Commodore Percival Drayton

Major General David Hunter

Thomas Fenwick Drayton at age 20

General T. F. Drayton and his brother Commodore Percival Drayton

Dress parade and review. First Regiment, South Carolina, (colored) Volunteers, Hilton Head.

General Robert E. Lee, in writing to his son Custis, December 29, 1861, from Coosawhatchie, South Carolina, observed, "The enemy is quiet and safe in his big boats. He is threatening everywhere around, pillaging, burning, and robbing where he can venture with impunity, and alarming women and children." Again he wrote on January 4, 1862, "Enemy quiet and retired to his Islands. The Main seemed too insecure for him, and he never went 400 yards from his steamers, not even to the extent of the range of his guns. After burning some houses (three) on the river bank, and feeling our proximity unpleasant, he retreated to Port Royal again."

On Hilton Head Island, the day of victory for the Union was a day of freedom for about 1,000 slaves who had elected to hide in the woods when their masters had fled their homes. Now these people, who were slowly beginning to understand the feeling that they were free to do as they pleased and who had been told the Yankees were devils, shyly came forth with food and information in exchange for hats and abandoned swords and souvenirs of battle. Soldiers found sweet potatoes in abundance in nearby fields. The Pope plantation house on Coggins Point was made the command post by the Federals.

Fortifications were quickly built from the northwest corner to the southeast tip along the mainland side in anticipation of a counterattack. Some of the earthworks were complete with moats and, as the garrisons had more time later, pets were made of the native alligators which were kept in these moats. Hunting and fishing provided a healthy diet, and General Sherman ordered the construction of a bakery of which he was inordinately proud. Why go out and look for trouble when life was so good right where they were? At night, under balmy skies, the troops could hear the former slaves singing and shouting in their Praise houses — the small wooden structures provided by the planters for the worship services of only a few slaves at a time, not enough space for large groups to gather, compare experiences and plot insurgence.

Meanwhile, General Lee, at Mrs. George Chisholm Mackey's house for headquarters, used the time to fortify the Coosawhatchie terminal midway between Charleston and Savannah. Beaufort, abandoned by its residents, had been occupied a month after Hilton Head. Coosawhatchie could be reached by steamboat. The Confederates there were outnumbered two to one and, according to Lee, they had "no guns which could resist their batteries." Lee had known the

Hilton Head General Sherman in the War with Mexico and was aware of his reluctance to fight. On April 20, 1862, forces were withdrawn from Pocotaligo towards Charleston, leaving that point on the railroad exposed. Still, General Sherman continued to walk the beach at Port Royal, inspect his bakery, and request more men and supplies.

The lone Union officer who wanted to take the war to the enemy was Colonel Isaac Ingalls Stevens, a seasoned and courageous soldier, who was stationed in Beaufort. All his efforts to persuade his general to pursue the rebels failed in spite of a complete campaign plan. If his plan had been followed, the war would have been shortened by years and saved thousands of lives. Certainly it would have lessened the bitterness of Reconstruction and the almost 100 years of hatred that prevailed in the South, a hatred that was not quelled until World War II brought Northern young men into Southern camps and dispelled the idea that "damnyankee" was one word.

At the time, General Sherman had other problems. Hundreds of slaves entered Federal lines and were in need of food, shelter, medicine and education. Sherman asked for agents to operate the abandoned plantations on Hilton Head and for teachers to educate the Negroes. The soldiers, unaware of these administrative problems and eager to fight Johnny Reb, called their general Old Granny Sherman. The General ordered the post office to be named Port Royal, official designation for the town of Hilton Head. It was not until 1872 that the name of the post office was restored to Hilton Head Island.

Colonel Stevens was also busy in Beaufort trying to restore order after the initial vandalism by slaves who masqueraded as their former masters and destroyed with a vengeance those very possessions that the slaves had been required to clean and polish. Beaufort had an extraordinary library, and Colonel Stevens tried to reassemble the volumes to their proper shelves. Twice General William Tecumseh Sherman sent personal orders that these valuable books be sent North. On the second order, acknowledging his superior officer, Colonel Stevens complied. The gallant and discouraged colonel was transferred in the summer of 1862 to Virginia and on September 1 died in the forefront of the second battle of Bull Run.

Some word must have reached Washington, however, for General Sherman was replaced by Major General David Hunter, a staunch abolitionist. But he, too, bent to the good life on Hilton Head Island, sent for his wife, practiced with his pistols on the beach and issued a proclamation, General Order No. 11, which astonished even President Lincoln. "...The persons in these three states — Georgia, Florida, and South Carolina — hertofore held as slaves are therefore declared forever free." The date was May 9, 1862, and President Lincoln was not nearly ready to declare emancipation, much less have one of his officers do so. Lincoln denied Hunter's call for freedom but allowed him to remain in command.

The garrison on Hilton Head was enjoying the surf and sun, gamboling and gambling. Buildings were going up at a rapid rate and the commerce from sea was interesting. About the only place that the realities of war were witnessed was in the big hospital that had been erected on the point at the Atlantic Ocean. Many wounded soldiers were brought there by boat, many died and were buried in the Union cemetery near the road which is now called Union Cemetery Road. Those interred were transferred a century later to the National Cemetery in Beaufort.

The name of Fort Walker was changed to Fort Welles to honor the Secretary of the Navy and later to Fort Sherman to honor its first commander. By Federal order in March, 1862, the Department of the South was announced with headquarters on Hilton Head.

A long wharf, complete with railroad track, allowed the largest ships to dock and load and unload the necessities of war and the luxuries of a thriving town that reached a population of 50,000 including army and navy personnel and the sutlers who supplied their needs. The large Port Royal House offered meals, rooms, and assorted ladies. Sutlers Row was known as Robbers Row, and history says it was well-deserved although newspaper editor Joseph H. Sears ran ads resembling those of New York stores in his Saturday morning paper, *The New South*. The butcher also dealt in under-the-counter whiskey, but only allowed one drink to a man. Bottles of whiskey could be bought at other stores along with imported perfumes and scented note papers which smelled nice but not nearly as nice as the bread coming from the bakery. Soldiers and sailors on Hilton Head could be photographed or tattooed on Sutlers Row.

Port Royal on Hilton Head Island had the largest number of permanent residents ever in its history. As a major supply depot dozens of ships entered Port Royal monthly with all sorts of cargo from Northern ports. Customs House officials were casual, and it followed that corrupt individuals would surreptitiously

Burial place and Light Ship at entrance to Port Royal Harbor

Fort Walker under bombardment by the United States Fleet November 7, 1861

The Marines landing to hoist the Stars and Stripes at Fort Walker

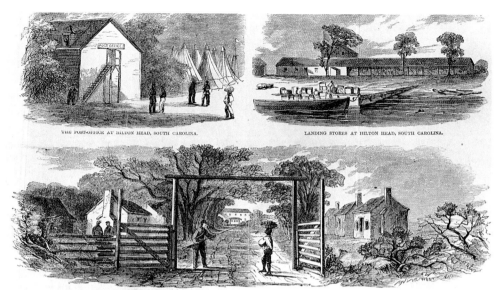

THE POST-OFFICE AT HILTON HEAD, SOUTH CAROLINA.

LANDING STORES AT HILTON HEAD, SOUTH CAROLINA.

OUR PICKET AT GENERAL DRAYTON'S MANSION, HILTON HEAD, SOUTH CAROLINA.—SKETCHED BY OUR SPECIAL ARTIST.—[SEE PAGE 779.]

Civil War Scenes

A dance given by General Gilmore at Hilton Head Island

fill boats for a night run to Confederate lines in Savannah where, in October 1862, quinine sold for $25 an ounce and opium was $40 a pound. Drugs, liquor, silks and corsets were loaded on Marsh Tackies, the sturdy Spanish steeds, by night and were off to Skull Creek for a boat trip to Savannah.

Early in the Civil War, April 11, 1862, Fort Pulaski which defended Savannah from the sea capitulated following a heavy bombardment from Admiral du Pont's Hilton Head-based ships. The blockade of one of two important Southern cities was complete. Prisoners and wounded were taken to Hilton Head to be transferred North later. Prisoners of war were kept in a large building; treatment at times was harsh and diet consisted of corn meal and onion pickles. Many men died and were buried in sandy graves. The blockade of Savannah was a great victory and the Hilton Head garrison was still celebrating at Thanksgiving, according to *The New South*, and soldiers bought turkeys, oysters, and vegetables from the enterprising former slaves. At Fort Pulaski, after a tremendous dinner, a shooting match was held with gold, silver, and bronze medals awarded to first, second, and third place riflemen. A rowing match followed on a mile-long course,

Government buildings for "Contrabands", (former slaves)

then a foot race, a hurdle sack race, and a wheelbarrow race. Newspaper editor Sears reported a special event for "the contrabands," as former slaves were called. The contestants, with hands tied behind their backs, were "to seize with their teeth a $5 gold piece dropped in a tub of meal." The third Negro to try, won.

About this time an unhappy event (for the contrabands) took place in Port Royal. The order went out for the muster of the first Negro troops into Federal service. In a diary kept by Susan Walker, a volunteer "missionary" to St. Helena Island from Wilmington, Massachusetts, she wrote, "Great excitement! Captain

Stevens brings orders from General Hunter that all colored men between 18 and 45 capable of bearing arms shall be taken to Hilton Head — no explanation. What can it mean? Are these men contrary to all American usages — United States usages rather — to be impressed *against will* to military service?" On another day she wrote, "house servants knew we were invited by M. Forbes to go to Hilton Head in his yacht, they were half afraid of our deserting them as their masters had done; that the Hilton Head excursion was but a pretext for escape. . . Early after breakfast Captain Stevens came with his soldiers to demand the men. I asked to be permitted to speak to them, when assembled, before he should give them his order. He did not give consent but ordered the soliders to load their guns in the very face of the assembled men and told them General Hunter had ordered them to Hilton Head, at the same moment ordering soldiers to fire on any one attempting to disobey the order of General Hunter. . . Women wept and children screamed as men were torn from their embrace. This is a sad day throughout these islands."

In spite of the impressed service of Negro males, Christmas of 1862, only one year after the defeat of Confederate forces on Hilton Head Island, was an exciting one for former slaves. They could buy land now with the money they had saved from selling to the soldiers and the army; their children could go to school; they had government housing near the fort; they could serve in the South Carolina Volunteers although they were "coerced" at bayonet point. In September of that year General Hunter had been replaced by General Ormsby M. Mitchel who would leave a strong memory on Hilton Head although he only lived four months after his arrival. Before he died of malaria, General Mitchel began construction of adequate Negro housing for several thousand homeless who had gathered on the Island since the start of the war. Government sawmills turned out pine siding and beams for barracks-like structures. Kitchens and wash houses were communal. The little town on the outskirts of Fort Walker (Welles) was named Mitchelville for the general. After General Mitchel's death, General Hunter was returned. (In 1987, extensive research and excavation of Mitchelville was funded and a report of these findings may be obtained through the Environmental and Historical Museum of Hilton Head Island.)

As has been stated, earthworks along the side of the Island facing the mainland were garrisoned shortly after the occupation. However, no threat seemed to be forthcoming from Confederate soldiers. Company H, 3rd New Hampshire, was sent on outpost duty to Pinckney Island and occupied the plantation house called The Point and another house three-quarters of a mile south. This plum seemed to be too ripe for the Confederates to resist. The Union company was soon captured in a raid led by Captain Stephen Elliott who had also commanded a landing party on Hilton Head the night after the surrender of Fort Walker and burned fourteen plantation houses to keep them from being used by the invaders. News of the successful foray on Pinckney Island and the capture of the Union soldiers was received at Hilton Head headquarters, but details were unavailable for six months when fourteen of the missing men found their way back to Hilton Head after being imprisoned in Columbia and in Richmond before being exchanged. In an anonymous account from one of the captured, he writes, "No insults were offered the men; but, on the contrary, a person meeting them might think the party had been out for pleasure. There were some fine singers among the rebels, and the air resounded with songs the whole day, and many a laugh went up on the conclusion of stories told by men on both sides. We were prisoners, but it was thought best to make the best of it."

This victory on Pinckney Island was probably not discussed at length, for events of larger scope were giving victories to the Union. One such incident took place in Charleston harbor and ended on Hilton Head Island. Robert Smalls, former slave, piloted the 140-foot steamer *Planter*, owned by a Charleston man, past three Confederate forts, including Fort Sumter, and into the hands of the Union fleet off Charleston, winning freedom for himself in the daring effort and

The U.S. Gunboats shelling the mainland opposite Port Royal Island

for his wife and children and a few "hands" aboard the *Planter*. They were delivered to Hilton Head where Smalls' piloting experience was recognized and used.

For the next two years life on Hilton Head remained routine and peaceful. A pattern of growth was established while elsewhere in the South hopes, homes and human lives were destroyed as battle after bloody battle seesawed across the once productive land. Mitchelville thrived, the theater excelled with full length plays, and the civilian/military population continued to grow until it could support a second newspaper, *The Palmetto Herald*.

Charles Nordhoff, writing for *Harper's New Monthly Magazine* in March, 1863, tells of Hilton Head Island abounding in roads and plantation houses, yellow jessamine, orange trees in bloom and of "the splendid magnolia beginning to flower." "The village of Hilton Head is a place which has grown up since the capture of the forts. . .The most prominent and ambitious building was originally a plantation house (Pope), to which has been added a curious superstructure — a tower — which is used as a signal station. The quarters of General Hunter and his staff front upon the water, and are simple enough to satisfy the demands of the most exacting democrat."

Thomas Dwight Howard, a young Harvard Divinity School graduate, ran five of the government operated plantations. His account reads: 12,000 acres planted in cotton in the 189 plantations in the Port Royal area around the Sound. All 25 Hilton Head plantations were worked with more than 9,000 people involved. As early as September, 1862, more than 30 schools operated in Beaufort-Port Royal district with 40 to 45 teachers instructing 2,000 children between the ages of eight and twelve.

The New England Freedmen's Aid Society's second annual report in April, 1864, reads, "The number of acres now owned by the freedmen is said to be not far from 7,350. More recently, at the sale of the town of Beaufort, from 75 to 80 houses and house lots were bought by the blacks, at prices ranging from $40 to $1,800. . ."

But life changed drastically on November 22, 1864, for the Hilton Head garrison with a message to Admiral Dahlgren who had replaced du Pont. Secretary of the Navy Gideon Welles instructed him as follows: "Major General (William Tecumseh) Sherman, with about 50,000 men, left Atlanta, Georgia, on the 16th instant, with the intention of reaching the Atlantic coast somewhere in the vicini-ty of Savannah. He may be expected about the middle of December, and the Department directs that you will be prepared to give him any needed coopera-tion that may be in your power."

This meant WAR for the soliders and sailors on Hilton Head Island. No more baseball on the beaches; no more horseback riding among the spreading oaks.

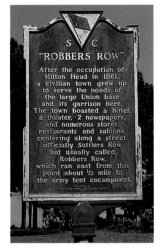
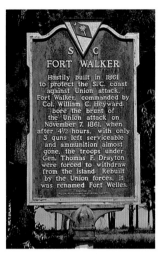

Historical markers on Fort Walker Road in Port Royal Plantation

Could they take the fresh-baked bread with them? This Sherman meant business, and his business was to break the back of the South and end this long and bloody war.

Rear Admiral John A. Dahlgren sent a naval detachment from Hilton Head on November 27 to assist in General Sherman's assault on Savannah. 160 sailors, 180 marines were on six shallow-draft gunboats that plied their way up the Broad River to rendezvous with land forces under General Foster's command. They landed eight miles from the Charleston-Savannah railroad which was still intact. A federal force of about 5,000 men had orders to sever the railroad line, burn bridges, and swing toward Savannah to meet Sherman.

Somehow things went astray as General Hatch's Union forces, on his orders, halted to build earthworks within one-half mile of the rendezvous point, los-ing the opportunity of surprise against the defending Confederates. Learning of this action through scouts, the battle-weary Confederates rallied men from Georgia, Columbia, Charleston, including cadets from The Citadel, a Charleston military college — a total of 1,400 infantry men and two detachments of cavalry. The men quickly assembled at a place called Honey Hill near Grahamville. Federal troops, not expecting any resistance, were marching in careless fashion up a dirt road right into the sights of a 12-pound cannon which the Confederates had hastily set up.

The action was hard fought from early morning until dark, and the Union losses were 746 killed, wounded or missing before the order to retreat was given. Confederate losses were 12 killed, 40 wounded in the Battle of Honey Hill, one of the last victories of the Confederacy. More than half the Federals were black troops, and an eyewitness account, passed on to a great-nephew in 1938, tells of many colored troops fallen on the battlefield, each with pockets full of money and a sprig of the herb called "Life Everlasting" in his cap.

On December 21 Sherman entered Savannah and sent his famous telegram to President Lincoln giving the President the city of Savannah for a Christmas present. Sherman stayed in Savannah for a month, allowing time for Confederate strength and morale to wear thin. On January 21, he wrote in his memoirs, "With my entire headquarters, officers, clerks, orderlies, etc., with wagons and horses, I embarked in a steamer for Beaufort, South Carolina, touching at Hilton Head to see General Foster.

While he was in Savannah, Sherman issued his Field Order #15 on January 16, 1865. This order reserved for negroes land from Charleston "to and including the lands bordering the St. John's River and the abandoned rice fields for 30 miles from the sea." A brilliant and short piece of writing. With a few words Sherman effectively deposited worrisome hordes who had accumulated behind his army as he marched across Georgia. He kept the possibility of anyone's owning many acres since one freedman could buy only ten acres and his wife could buy ten. Sherman made certain that, by dividing up the land into small parcels, no one person could accumulate large portions and become land barons once again.

Sherman's march on Columbia and Charleston began January 25. He was determined to punish ruthlessly that state which was the first to secede from the Union and which had first fired on Fort Sumter, beginning this Civil War. Both cities fell on the same day, February 17.

Increasing numbers of prisoners were sent to Hilton Head, 600 of whom had been captured when Savannah forts fell. The prison was near the beach in the broiling sun. In a stockade measuring 50 square yards, in cells measuring six by seven feet and occupied by four to nine officers, conditions were grim with each prisoner allowed one pint of stale meat, four ounces of bread and the ever-present pickle. The prison had one door and no windows. Prisoners were locked in at 5 o'clock in the afternoon and were not allowed outside into the stockade until seven the next morning.

When Robert E. Lee surrendered at Appomatox and the War was over, Federal troops were withdrawn from Hilton head Island, although the land still belonged to the United States government. Only the Mitchelville inhabitants remained and as the years drifted on, they stripped the hospital and post office and other buildings of planks and beams to build dwellings for themselves on land that they owned and farmed with pride. It was the beginning of 100 years of peace on a beautiful island which was almost forgotten.

HILTON HEAD

When Carolina's recreant sons
Flung out their flags and charged their guns
And in their boasting, haughty pride
Their Country and her laws defied,

From far out o'er the water line
A cloud was lifting from the brine
That nearer came and took such form
They trembled at the coming storm.

But still they stood and dared the worst,
And soon the gathering storm-cloud burst,
An never were such death drops shed
Before, on haughty Hilton Head.

Yet Southern Chivalry could not
Withstand the storm of shell and shot,
But seized with terror broke and fled
Ingloriously from Hilton Head,

But not until the deadly boom
Had sealed full many a traitor's doom;
Though sad, we have no tears to shed
For those who fell on Hilton Head.

Alas! It was a sore defeat;
The northern "mudsills" from our fleet
Hauled down their flag and raised instead
The Stars and Stripes on Hilton Head.

Now in Port Royal's safe retreat,
Securely rides that gallant fleet,
And none but traitors now need dread,
The frowning forts on Hilton Head.

by Robert Willamson
Light Co E, 3rd U.S. Artillery
September 22, 1863

CHAPTER X
The Sleeping Beauty

As years passed, time stood still for the 3,000 Negroes still on Hilton Head Island. The sea took the Elliott house at Myrtle Bank and the large General Hospital at Port Royal. Sherman's Field Order #15 assured that there would no longer be large landholders or reclamation of entire plantations by former owners. But even while Union forces occupied Hilton Head Island, confiscated land was put up for sale. Spec-

"W.P. Clyde acquired, piece-by-piece, 9,000 acres and made the Honey Horn House, the only usable ante-bellum house, his own."

ulators, resident teachers and supervisors grabbed at the opportunity to buy this fabulous paradise for a dollar an acre, or perhaps a dollar and a quarter with house, barns, tools, and livestock thrown in.

With money hoarded from earnings as laborers or provisioners to the Yankees, freed slaves stepped forward and plunked down hard cash. Sales opened as early as December 1, 1863. The very next day, 1,000 acres of Honey Horn Plantation sold for $200. The following February it was re-sold for $10,000. The land boom was short-lived, however. Failure to propagate long-staple cotton by the proven Elliott method and abandonment of the rice crop caused land prices to fall to $15 an acre.

Gullah was the spoken language of the islands. The occupying forces despaired of ever conversing or understanding this strange and beautiful dialect, but at last the freedmen could speak and sing among themselves without being a curiosity and without taking orders from anyone. Gullah has been defined as a blend of the slaves' native African cadence and the Elizabethan English of the West Indies at the time of colonization. As the slaves tilled fields in the West Indies and were conversing in their native African tongue interspersed with a few English phrases, they were asked what language they were speaking. When they responded, "Angollan," the word became corrupted into "Gullah." The story is told of a Gullah soldier stationed in North Africa during World War II. Most of the men thought he was from South Africa because they couldn't understand him. A Southerner came along, talked with the Gullah and advised his fellow soldiers that the man was a full-blooded American G.I.

In 1874 Carbetbagger W. D. Brown bought 500-acre Folly Field for $110, and the 40-acre Grasslawn went to William Wilson for $90. Much later, Brown and his wife were murdered, robbed, and their house burned to the ground, not by Islanders but by visitors who came by boat.

By 1890, when the Island was almost forgotten, word was again circulated in Northern circles of the salubrious climate and abundance of game. The hunters returned. A Beaufort hunting club bought 1,000 acres in Leamington Plantation (Palmetto Dunes) and later sold it to the North Carolina Hunt Club which doubled the size of their preserve. W. P. Clyde acquired, piece-by-piece, 9,000 acres and made the Honey Horn house, the only usable ante-bellum house, his own. The Federal government held on to (and probably forgot about) their 803 acres at Fort Walker.

Of course, hunting activities were only seasonal and most of the time the Negro landowners became subsistence farmers and fishermen, or both. The Marsh Tackey was hitched to the plow on weekdays and to the wagon on Sundays. Kitchen chairs were set up in back of the wagon and the family went to church which lasted most of the day. Other than the religious experience, church was both a social and political gathering place. In 1895 the South Carolina constitutional convention disenfranchised the Black population, and the Blacks became necessarily self-governing with the Baptist chuch becoming the single most important force in their lives. Politics in the pulpit was born and has continued in spite of the fact that today Blacks vote and hold office.

In a subsistence society currency was hard to come by, but the close-knit Island community bartered their goods and their attentions. Any surplus farm goods were loaded on the boat which traveled the intercoastal waters between Savannah and Beaufort to be sold in town at the markets. The boat made two stops on Hilton Head: Long Island (Calibogue Cay) and Jenkins Island (Windmill Harbour). Doors were never locked, for crime did not exist among Islanders. As one ancient resident of Beach City (near Mitchelville) said, "You could park a wagon loaded with gold at the crossroads overnight, and no one would touch it."

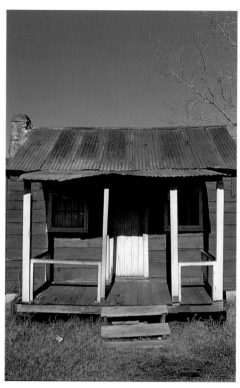

The Leamington light house in 1969

A typical home of the period

Remains of the steam cannon in Port Royal Plantation

World War II gun bases on Palmetto Dunes beach.

The new lodge which burned down in the 1970s

The original Hurley hunting lodge about 1920

Mrs. Hurley's favorite portrait of
W. L. Hurley

A hunting party ready to start out at Hilton Head Island.

This 1873 map shows that original roads followed much the same route as today's roads.

In 1893 a devastating hurricane struck and a tremendous wave inundated all the sea islands from Savannah to North Edisto inlet, killing an estimated 1,000 people. Property damage was estimated at $10 million at that time. Joel Chandler Harris, author of the Uncle Remus stories, was sent to Port Royal by *Scribner's Magazine*, and he wrote (with a degree of exaggeration), ". . . near 3,000 people drowned, between 20 and 30,000 human beings without means of subsistence. . ." No warning systems were possible then, and with the constant yearly threat of hurricanes, the daily battle with disease and hardships, the isolation, the nation wondered, "Why do they stay?" Mr. Harris wrote of a woman who was going back to Hilton Head following the storm. In answer to the question, she answered in Gullah, "You smell de ma'sh when you'n young — you mus' smell 'im when you ol' — enty?" ("Enty" is the Gullah's brief for "You understand?")

As the United States marked the end of the 19th century, the Spanish American War caused Congress to authorize the building of seven pneumatic dynamite guns, or "steam cannons." One of these "cannons" was built near the site of the Confederate Fort Walker and was tested in 1901 with the results on file in the National Archives. During the procedure the gun was fired 53 times, not once or twice as island legend has reported. A complete report is on file at the Museum of Hilton Head Island. The ruins of the concrete emplacement are still visible at the Port Royal Plantation beach.

In 1899 W. L. Hurley bought Otter Hole plantation and lived in its house on a grand scale with his yacht docked in front on Broad Creek, and an automobile parked in his back yard. He also acquired Muddy Creek and Gardner's plantations, bringing his total acreage to 1,700. In the late 1960s, the Hurley House was turned into a night club, unsuccessfully, and mysteriously burned to the ground not long after opening.

In 1931 Landon K. Thorne and Alfred L. Loomis determined to buy as much of Hilton Head Island as possible for hunting purposes and even succeeded in acquiring all of the Fort Walker site from the United States government for $12,600. By this time the Black population had dropped to 300. Those seeking broader opportunities looked elsewhere for education and jobs. Others, particularly among the elders, were unhappy with all the Northerners come to buy their land. Hilton Head Islanders loved their home and could not understand why Northerners could not love their own homes as well. "Den dey would neber come here to buy all away from we."

During World War II the turn-of-the-century lighthouse in Palmetto Dunes was the site of Camp McDougal, used by the Shore Patrol. Near the base of the lighthouse several buildings served the needs of the personnel. Two of those buildings were lighthouse-keepers houses. As the conception of Harbour Town germinated in Charles Fraser's mind, he bought the lighthouse-keeper houses and moved them to Harbour Town where they were restored and have since been used by various businesses. Gun emplacements, for target practice out over the Atlantic Ocean, were built on the Palmetto Dunes beach. With the ebb and flow of both tides and sands, these rounded concrete slabs may occasionally be seen just south of the Hyatt Hotel.

Were the times better then for the 300 permanent inhabitants of the Island or did they need job opportunities that would allow the young people to return, did they need better medical care, more sanitary living conditions that would come with the resort development of Hilton Head Island? That is a question that has been argued from 1950 to the present day, for 1950 marks the beginning of the Modern Age for the sea islands, a time when Beaufort County began its upward climb out of the poverty pocket where it had been for more than a century.

The blue trim on early houses is believed to ward off evil.

CHAPTER XI
The Modern Age

*H*ilton Head shook itself free of its somnambulance in 1950 when Georgia natives bought 19,000 of the Island's 25,000 acres for over a million dollars. Charles Fraser, a young law student, and Fred Hack, a timberman, together with General Joseph B. Fraser (Charles' father), C. C. Stebbins (Hack's father-in-law) and Olin McIntosh dared to forego timbering the

"In 1956 a two-lane drawbridge, named for South Carolina's famous son James F. Byrnes, was dedicated."

great forests and sell the land once again to pleasure seekers.

When Charles Fraser first explored the forests and swamps, having arrived by mail boat, *Alligator II*, there was only one paved road which ran from the boat dock on Jenkins Island to the site of the World War II shore patrol encampment at Palmetto Dunes. He recalls only eleven cars and trucks, about 100 Marsh Tackies, no electricity, no telephones and no medical facilities. Fraser tells us in his publication, *The Art of Community Building*, "Hilton Head and Daufuskie were far more isolated in 1950 than they had been between 1836 and 1940." During that period steam excursion/freight/mail boats made regular runs and stops from Savannah to Charleston and return, stopping on signal at two places on Hilton Head Island — a dock on Calibogue Cay (then called Long Island) and on Jenkins Island. An inhabitant of Hilton Head since birth was asked what, for her, was the single biggest event in the modern development of the Island. Without hesitation her response was, "The day they turned on the electricity." The year was 1951.

Diverse dispositions caused two development companies to be formed, with the Frasers taking the South end of the Island to begin Sea Pines Plantation and the Hack faction the North, spawning Port Royal Plantation. As Charles Fraser unrolled vast plans before investors, no one realized they were witnessing a basic land system that would become the prototype for all other successful developments. Fraser recalls a "glorious era at which architects outnumbered real estate salesmen on the Island three to one."

A major part of the grand plan was a number of golf courses around which lots could be planned, but no playground can prosper without access for the players. In 1953 the South Carolina Highway Department supplied a six-car ferry that ran from Buckingham Landing to the dock on Jenkins Island. In 1956 a two-lane drawbridge, named for South Carolina's famous son James F. Byrnes, was dedicated. Users were charged a toll of $2.50 per car. A large majority of people crossing the bridge said the Island "would never go" because the obstacles seemed to outweigh the overwhelming beauty of the beaches. Mostly dirt roads followed the same paths as plantation roads of the Golden Age. The only paved ones showed beach property which sold readily. It was twenty years before land sales would truly soar and the developments, called Plantations, could be called flourishing.

One of the significant obstacles to overcome was the tiny mosquito. Due to many small, shallow ponds, the Island was a great breeding ground for mosquitoes as well as alligators. Alligators were no problem except to small dogs and pigs, but the mosquitoes were delivering up to forty bites per minute. Through the efforts of a Columbia, South Carolina, entomologist, Dr. Frank Arnold, the crisis was solved and the Island became comfortably habitable.

A year after the James F. Byrnes Crossing was complete, Wilton Graves opened the ten-room Sea Crest Motel, each room with a lock but no key. Mr. and Mrs. Louis McKibben were the innkeepers, and Mr. McKibben directed guests to take a short walk down the beach to his new Arcade which had a refrigerator stocked with necessities and a stove. You were welcome to cook your own breakfast. The only other place on the Island to eat was Mrs. Katie McElveen's Roadside Restaurant where visitors and a few residents could enjoy a "special" of fresh vegetables, meat, cornbread and very, very sweet iced tea while observing a painting of the Last Supper on velvet.

Telephones were installed in 1960. Prior to that, notes were left at front doors, on bulletin boards scattered about the Island, and emergencies were solved via mobile phones. The Sea Pines Plantation Company, which had its offices in a glorified trailer, had a telephone in a most unusual booth — a derelict automobile behind the offices.

Harbour Town in 1969

Harbour Town 19 years later

The Hilton Head Inn

Early directional sign

The Pope Avenue branch of the U.S. Post Office, opened in 1966

Former Sea Pines Plantation Company sales office at Sea Pines Circle

Medical services came to the Island in the mid-1960s with the building of a medical center and the persuasion of Dr. Chester Goddard to become its first doctor. This was also the time, in 1965, when *Islander* magazine was first published.

About this time the lone figure who was to make such a difference to the descendants of those former slaves came to Hilton Head. She is Charlotte Heinrichs, a nurse who never retired. Those fortunate enough to live within developments with their sophisticated infrastructures enjoyed sweet and pure water from deep wells and indoor plumbing. Others who had lived all their lives on the island had only shallow wells and outside pumps. Disease and internal parasites go hand in hand with such situations. Mrs. Heinrichs single handedly spearheaded the Deep Well Project which brought sanitary conditions to all Islanders. Although in her eighties when the task was completed, she continued to collect food, clothing and furnishings for destitute people.

In 1969 two important events began on Hilton Head Island, one still celebrated every year and the other almost entirely forgotten. The annual "party" that has done so much for the Island in national news is the Heritage Golf Classic on the Harbour Town Links. The population was recorded as 2,500 and yet hosted a gallery of 5,000 people. Of the 2,500 permanent residents, about 50 banded together to make national news on another front, the one almost forgotten. On October 2, 1969, 1,822 acres at Victoria Bluff on the mainland near Moss Creek was sold to Badische Anilin-und-Sodafabrick for a chemical complex. Negotiations for the sale by the South Carolina Port Authority had been kept secret by state representatives. When the sale and intentions of the purchasing company were made public, Hilton Head environmentalists, under the leadership of Franklin O. Rouse, rose up to stop the giant BASF. Hilton Head Island has been called the Bunker Hill in a national War Against Pollution, and all media covered the fight of little David against the Giant. On April 7, 1970, BASF officials announced their decision to Interior Secretary Walter Hickel to suspend construction at the site.

The decade beginning 1970 marked the change from gradual development to rapid growth. Jonathan Daniels, Ralph Hilton, and Tom Wamsley started a 12-page tabloid newspaper, *The Island Packet*. In 1973, supports for the James F. Byrnes drawbridge were struck by a runaway barge, and traffic was suspended for a month while repairs were made. Until the Corps of Engineers completed a pontoon bridge, the local Coast Guard Auxiliary quickly went into action and supplied the island with daily needs. Helicopter service took emergency cases to Savannah and Beaufort hospitals. Local leaders immediately began lobbying for a higher, stationary span with four lanes. Earlier that same year the first Family Circle Magazine tennis cup was held in Sea Pines, and polo returned to this area at Honey Horn Plantation. Nearby Pinckney Island was given as a permanent nature preserve by the owners, Edward Starr, Jr. and James Barker.

Commemorative plaque on Highway 278 across from Moss Creek Plantation

The Hilton Head Dock

A young New York orthopedic surgeon, Dr. Peter LaMotte, docked his boat at Harbour Town while traveling down the Intracoastal Waterway. The more he saw of Hilton Head Island, the better he liked it. He immediately ascertained the need for a hospital, gathered a legion of followers, and in 1975 a hospital superior to most was completed. The resident population had grown to 6,500.

It is good to recall that, since the turn of the century, Hilton Head Island was a place that had nothing except its considerable natural resources. After the storm and tidal wave of 1893, nothing but a few foundations were left standing except the damaged buildings at Honey Horn Plantation. Builders, businesses, and other citizens were required to make this an island acceptable to those who would be "well transported thither." Fred Hack gave property for the First Presbyterian Church and the library, and Charles Fraser donated land along Pope Avenue for Episcopal, Methodist, and Roman Catholic churches, as well as acreage for the Sea Pines Forest Preserve and the Newhall Reserve. Services taken for granted in most communities were needed, banks, lawyers, insurance companies, grocery stores, to name but a few. As the population grew to 10,776 in 1980 and doubled by 1988, incorporation into the Town of Hilton Head became necessary in the eyes of the majority. These relatively few people were servicing the needs, both real and imagined, of up to five times their number in tourism as nearly all major hotels built here.

The winter of 1984-1985 was a season of vast changes for both residents and developers on Hilton Head Island. The changes can be summed up in two words: Bobby Ginn. In a matter of weeks the 36-year-old entrepreneur had persuaded savings and loan institutions from out of state to lend him millions of dollars and this South Carolina native swept almost half the Island acreage into his portfolio. Sea Pines Plantation, Port Royal Plantation, Shipyard, Wexford, Indigo Run — all came under his control. Promises were sent up like smoke signals and vanished just as quickly. A year later Bobby Ginn was bankrupt and the people who attempted to bail him out introduced an element to Hilton Head Island heretofore not experienced. John Curry was appointed to sort out the shambles and to try and smooth over the bad publicity attached to bankruptcy. Investors hesitated to buy land or homes. Unwanted, a moratorium on building existed simply because people were afraid to take a chance. By 1988, property owners in Sea Pines Plantation and Wexford bought the developments and outside interests retrieved the rest.

Chapters are written every day in the History of Hilton Head Island. The census has yet to record as many Islanders as were here in 1863. Will this island become, as many predict, the largest town in the state of South Carolina? Hilton Head Island has helped tremendously in the the economic expansion of the state. In any case, it will be the people who have chosen to live here that will make the difference, for better or worse, on Hilton Head Island.

This marker has been erected as a lasting tribute
to the following men who envisioned
Hilton Head Island
as a place where man could commune
with Nature and enjoy the Sea and the Sky,
the good Earth and the Forest and all things
that dwell therein.
These men determined that no "Fayrer or Fytter"
place should be found than on Hilton Head Island
where man could live in peace and solitude
for a day or a life time:
General Joseph B. Fraser   Olin T. McIntosh, Sr.
Fred C. Hack   C. C. Stebbins
and to those men who have
continued the high ideals of these Pioneers
we pause to salute and reflect
on what man has wrought.
ERECTED THIS 6th DAY OF NOVEMBER, 1969, BY
THE BANK OF BEAUFORT HISTORIC FOUNDATION

Commemorative plaque located at The Anchor Bank on Pope Avenue

SOURCES

Hilton Head, A Sea Island Chronicle by Virginia C. Holmgren (1959), Hilton Head Island Publishing Company.

Port Royal Under Six Flags by Katharine M. Jones (1960) Bobbs-Merril.

Department of the South by Robert Carse (1961) The State Printing Company.

Tales of Ante Bellum Hilton Head Island Families by Rev. Robert E. H. Peeples (1970).

Plantations of the Low Country by William P. Baldwin, Jr., (1985) Legacy Publications, Greensboro, North Carolina

Indian and Freedmen Occupation at the Fish Haul Site (38BU805) Beaufort County, South Carolina. Chicora Foundation Research Series 7.

Archaeological Survey of Hilton Head Island, South Carolina, Research Series 9, by Michael Trinkley. Chicora Foundation.

The Art of Community Building by Charles E. Fraser (1988).

Exploring Our Lost Century by Joseph Judge. National Geographic, March 1988.

The Short, Unhappy Life of a Maverick Caribbean Colony by Charles R. Ewen, *Archaeology* magazine, July/August 1988.